Job Interviews In A Week

Alison Straw is an independent consultant and executive coach. Her career has been devoted to helping individuals, groups and organizations develop. She is passionate about engaging and inspiring people and has worked with many senior executives, supporting them in developing themselves, their careers and their organizations. She has co-authored *Tackling Tough Interview Questions* and *Successful Networking*.

Mo Shapiro, a partner at INFORM T&C, is a master practitioner in NLP and coaching. She has an outstanding record as a communications and presentation skills coach and trainer and an international public speaker. Mo contributes regularly to all broadcast media, has authored *Successful Interviewing* and *Neuro-linguistic Programming* and co-authored *Tackling Tough Interview Questions*.

Teach Yourself®

Job Interviews In A Week

Alison Straw
and
Mo Shapiro

Also available in ebook

Contents

Introduction

Have you ever wondered why some people seem to succeed almost effortlessly whenever they go for an interview? Perhaps they are just 'lucky'. We think not! Their performance, and ultimately their success, is the result of thorough personal preparation.

You, too, can improve your ability and success through a combination of thought, training, practice and experience. This book is your companion in the process. By setting time aside to read a chapter each day over the course of a week, you will be guided on your route to success:

- **Sunday** – Understand the interview process so you know what to expect.
- **Monday** – Do your research on the interview, the role and the organization so you can demonstrate your knowledge of their requirements.
- **Tuesday** – Discover what differentiates you to make yourself the memorable candidate.
- **Wednesday** – Prepare yourself for success to feel confident in the interview.
- **Thursday** – Respond skilfully and be prepared for interviewers' questions and exercises.
- **Friday** – Decide what questions you want to ask, to demonstrate being proactive.
- **Saturday** – Put it all together and know that you have done all you can towards your success.

Since writing the first edition of *Succeeding At Interviews In A Week*, we have been challenged by individuals and situations which have made us stop and consider how best to prepare readers for these questions. We have continued to talk to people who have succeeded at interviews and consulted colleagues who regularly interview. All this accumulated knowledge and experience is contained within this book.

You are now making the first significant investment in improving your interview performance to increase your chances of getting the job you want – congratulations! Now read on ... and good luck!

Alison Straw
and
Mo Shapiro

SUNDAY

What to expect from the interview process

You opened the post this morning to find you have been invited to an interview – great news! You feel good. You are high, elated and you congratulate yourself. You imagine yourself in the role; it's exciting, an ideal job for you. You read the letter again and, as the reality of the interview becomes your focus, you are bombarded with less positive feelings and thoughts, such as:

- I hate interviews.
- I can't remember the last time I was interviewed.
- I really want this job – I hope I don't let myself down.

It is not uncommon to feel a degree of trepidation in anticipation of an interview. The trick is not to let this weigh you down.

After all, we suspect you've experienced being interviewed, not just once but many times in your career. Most career transitions – such as selection, promotion or other forms of career development – will have been punctuated by interviews. You are therefore likely to be familiar with the process. As interviews follow a relatively common format, you will already have some of the skills and knowledge required to make you successful. Today we look at how to use this experience in your next interview.

Learning from past interviews

Think back over past interviews and answer the following question honestly: *Did I present myself in the best possible light?*

While we would hope that your answer is 'yes', it is more likely to be 'no' or 'not quite'. Even if, as a manager, you are an experienced interviewer, having undergone training on skills, techniques and questioning, you may not be so skilled at being interviewed.

Take some time now to think about some of your previous experiences as an interviewee. Think firstly about those where you have been less successful; what happened and what can you learn from them? What would you do differently if you encountered a similar situation? Note or record your findings. Now think about your successful interviews. What did you do that led to a positive outcome and what can you repeat when you go along to your next interview?

The following comments from interviewers reflect common problems:

- I know a lot about his employer, but very little about him.
- She seemed very nervous and aggressive.
- He stumbled over all the questions related to his personality.
- I'm not sure how long he would stay.
- She seemed too good to be true.
- There was no substance in what he said.
- It was difficult to get a word in edgeways.

SUNDAY
MONDAY
TUESDAY
WEDNESDAY
THURSDAY
FRIDAY
SATURDAY

Having had experiences of being interviewed and being the interviewer, you will be aware that interviews often follow a tried and tested pattern. Today, we will help you focus on the known rather than the unpredictable factors, exploring questions such as why, in what way and by whom:

● Why: interview objectives
● In what way: types of questions
● By whom: the interviewer or interviewers

Interview objectives

If you have been invited to an interview – well done! Your invitation is based on the limited knowledge the interviewer has of you from your application, a previous telephone interview, personal recommendation or your past achievements. They already believe that you could be the person they are looking for. The interview is therefore an opportunity for interviewers to extend their knowledge and complete their picture of you.

You will have your own agenda. The interview is an opportunity for you to discover further information about the job and the organization. Based on that information, you can reach decisions about match and suitability.

The interview is a two-way process: treat it as such.

The interviewee's objectives are to:

● progress to the next stage and the final shortlist
● gain the initiative – an offer or a commitment
● present yourself in the best possible light
● make known your talents and expertise
● fill gaps in your knowledge about the job and the organization
● meet future colleagues/managers
● be clear about whether or not you would accept the post.

The interviewer's objectives are to:

● find the most suitable person
● encourage you to express yourself fully
● look for specific skills and achievements

- sell the job and the organization
- assess your initial impact and social fit
- appoint the right person.

You will both have independent objectives with a degree of overlap. Spend time before the interview clarifying your objectives. You may even want to rank them; having gone through this process, you can be much clearer about whether the interview matches your objectives and, if not, for what reason.

Interview structure

The whole of the recruitment process requires careful planning. It involves drawing up a job description and person specification, designing the advertisement, compiling the information pack, and then selecting who to interview and shortlist. The interview itself must also be carefully planned.

Be aware that interviewers will have clarified their objectives in general and decided on a format and a set of questions for each interviewee. No two interviews are the same. Your personality, application, CV, and experience will be different from others', as will the areas that require further exploration because they are of particular interest or concern. While interviews are not the same, there are similarities, and there is a process which is common and accepted.

The process can be likened to a sandwich. It is built on some 'warm-up' questions to help you both settle down and feel as comfortable as you can.

The middle and main section of the interview will constitute the filling in the sandwich, the most important ingredients, where you will be asked a variety of questions, checking and clarifying match and suitability.

In the final stage there will be time for your questions, closing with a summary of the interview and an indication of what will happen next: a second interview, a meeting with other staff members, or a letter telling you the result of the interview.

Some organizations provide their interviewers with a standard form to assess certain aspects of the interviewee and their performance. They will have a rating scale for each competence and make direct comparisons between candidates. Depending on the post available, these may cover the following:

- skills
- knowledge
- behaviour
- motivation
- fit with team
- fit with culture
- career aspirations.

Types of question

During your interview you will encounter a number of different types of question. If you can recognize these and the reasons they are being asked, you can concentrate on your replies. We will give you further guidance on responding to questions on Thursday.

The better the questions, the better the interview. Questions can be categorized as follows:

- open
- probing
- closed
- hypothetical
- leading
- difficult
- negative
- discriminatory.

Open questions

These are where interviewers give you the chance to talk. They want to hear your ideas and see how you develop an answer. Open questions usually start with:

'Who', 'What', 'Where', 'When', 'Which', 'Why' or 'How'.

For example:

- 'What levels of budget responsibility have you had throughout your career?'
- 'How did you implement your people strategy?'

Questions such as these allow you the opportunity to sell yourself. They require a level of preparation on your part. Think about the key themes that are likely to be covered in the interview, focusing on those which you consider will be of interest to the interviewer and most relevant to the job.

Probing questions

When interviewers are particularly interested in your reply and want further information, they will use probing questions to focus in on the subject.

For example:

- 'Tell me about your research to date.'
- 'How did you manage the change?'
- 'What made you respond in that way?'

It's rather like a funnelling process where the interviewer moves from general questions to specific examples.

Closed questions

These are direct questions that tend to pin you down to a factual reply or to a 'yes' or 'no' answer.

For example:

- 'Were you responsible for managing a budget in your last job?'
- 'Are you familiar with Investors in People?'

Questions such as these can inhibit you and restrict your freedom in presenting information. For example, you may not have been responsible for the budget in your last post, but you may have had budget responsibilities in the past. If you are not able to communicate this information, it may reduce your chances of being successful. Always try to highlight relevant previous experience. Just because an interviewer asks a closed question, it doesn't mean they only want a one-word answer. Use your initiative and be prepared to provide a fuller answer.

Hypothetical questions

Hypothetical questions are just that, encouraging you to imagine how you might handle the unknown. They also provide an opportunity for you to demonstrate how well you think and the quality of your judgement. The interviewer will suggest a hypothetical situation and ask how you would deal with it.

For example:

- 'What would you do if ... ?'
- 'How would you deal with ... ?'
- 'What would you expect from a perfect manager?'

These can tend to be difficult questions to answer, especially if complex scenarios are being presented. If you are not careful, you can end up tying yourself in knots, especially if you concentrate too much on trying to work out what kind of answer you think they might want. Try to relate these questions to your own experience and, if you are not clear about the complete details of the situation, ask for more information.

Leading questions

These are the opposite of hypothetical questions, as the interviewer steers you to the kind of answer they expect.

Leading questions do not give interviewers much of an idea about you, though you will have an insight into their thinking. Generally it is best not to rock the boat; go where the questions are leading and check if you are unclear.

For example:

- 'As you have had experience of budgeting, I'm sure you wouldn't ...'
- 'With regard to Investors in People, you are obviously aware of the problems with ...'

Difficult questions

These take many shapes and forms. Give yourself a moment to think, rather than trying to start answering immediately. Don't be evasive; you may have some ideas about areas of questioning that are likely to cause you difficulty.

Anticipate what areas interviewers might cover and be ready for them. It is important to have some kind of answer ready rather than clamming up and leaving interviewers to jump to their own, possibly incorrect, conclusions.

For example:

- 'I see you have a gap of three years in your employment. What did you do during that time?'
- 'This job requires a professional diploma. How are you going to make up the shortfall in your qualifications?'

You don't know which questions will take you by surprise. Whatever they are, take your time over them. And remember that, in most cases, the interviewer is trying to give you the opportunity to put yourself forward in the best possible light, not trying to trip you up.

Negative questions

Don't let negative questions unnerve you; they may be the interviewer's way of making comparisons between the best candidates.

For example:

● 'What are your weaknesses?'
● 'Why is it that you have changed jobs so often?'
● 'You stayed in your last job for ten years. Why so long?'

Don't fall into the trap of defending yourself, as though this were a direct attack. Be constructive and turn the question around to show yourself in a positive light.

Discriminatory questions

These sorts of questions are still asked at interview, particularly of women and minority groups.

Women applying for senior jobs may be confronted with a whole battery of questions about their private lives, which male colleagues might not be asked.

For example:

● 'How does your husband feel about you applying for this post?'

- 'What effect might the increased responsibility have on your family life?'
- 'Are you planning to have a family?'

People from minority groups may be asked, for example:

- 'How would you respond to criticism from a white colleague?'

These all need to be handled very carefully. You need to clarify the interviewer's intention and the relevance of the question. Ask yourself and maybe even the interviewer:

- 'Is this question ever put to other candidates?'
- 'How would this affect my performance in the role?'

It could be that the interviewer is just clumsy rather than malicious.

If you feel that you have been discriminated against in your interview, in the UK you can contact the Equality Advisory & Support Service (EASS).

FREEPOST Equality Advisory & Support Service
FPN4431
Telephone: (+44) (0)808 800 0082
www.equalityadvisoryservice.com

In the USA you should contact:
US Equal Employment Opportunity Commission (EEOC)
131 M Street, NE
Washington DC 20507-0100
Telephone: (+1) 800 669 4000
www.eeoc.gov

In Commonwealth countries you should contact:
Commonwealth Secretariat
Marlborough House
Pall Mall
London SW1Y 5HX
UK
Telephone: (+44) (0)20 7747 6500
www.thecommonwealth.org

As well as recognizing the different types of question, it is worth considering the order in which the questions are asked. The use of supplementary and probing questions will often suggest what is in the interviewer's mind; you should notice this and react accordingly.

Good interviewers will be watching your reactions and body language: posture, gestures and facial expressions. You should do the same; some interviewers present an unresponsive, wooden mask. This can be because they are inexperienced or are not comfortable with the role. With practice, you should be able to read and assess intentions and reactions reasonably well. You will undoubtedly also meet some ineffective interviewers.

Interviewers

Simply by putting yourself in the shoes of the interviewer you can begin to see things from their perspective. You can appreciate the investment they've made in the process, the importance of making the right decision or, conversely, the cost of making a wrong decision. Of course, you will have your own objectives and we are assuming you want to get the job, but we suggest that the interview is your final exploration of the role, the expectations and the organization.

Bear in mind, though, that good interviewers are trained, not born. Be prepared for an interviewer who:

● has not read your CV
● gets aggressive, to see how you react under stress
● is constantly distracted
● responds to texts or emails during the interview
● makes remarks about your previous employer or boss
● asks questions but doesn't listen to your answers.

Even the best training can fall on deaf ears and even the best interviewers can have a bad day. If you happen to be on the receiving end of poor interviewing, you can sometimes turn it to your advantage. You may meet interviewers who fall into the following categories.

The disorganized interviewer

Allow them time to settle down and find the papers or notes they need. Establish your preparedness early on and, if necessary, subtly suggest an interview structure.

The unprepared interviewer

Sometimes very experienced interviewers think they can sail in on the day and don't need to prepare. You have to keep calm and be patient. It won't do your cause any good if you try to catch them out or show them up. If interviewers have a position of authority over the post, you may want to consider how you would feel working with them.

The nervous interviewer

You sense that the interviewer would rather be anywhere else than in an interview room and may even be more nervous than you are. This sometimes happens when specialist functional managers are taken out of their familiar work setting and expected to be at ease in a more social setting. They will be grateful if you offer relevant information and loosely control the interview. Be careful not to patronize.

The aggressive interviewer

Don't allow aggressive interviewers to provoke you. Rather than apologizing for the weaknesses, failings or gaps in your CV that they point out to you, give positive explanations and put over what you have prepared.

Being familiar with the process of the interview will enable you to understand the direction it is taking. If you are unclear about a question, try to assess what the reasons are for asking it and answer it accordingly.

The well-informed interviewer

It is now common practice for interviewers to gather information from a variety of sources. You should be prepared for questions on what you have posted on social networking sites, as recruiters may have done their research well.

 TIP *Be cautious about what you post and the privacy levels you set, as these could trip you up at interview. The last thing you need at interview are probing questions about a recent party you attended.*

Summary

We have begun this week with a general overview of the process of interviews, preparing you for what you should expect.

Interviews come in a variety of forms – so you have to enter the process with an open mind. In recent years, practice in many organizations has become more sophisticated. Interviewers are more extensively trained; they are given a set of developed questions for different roles or a battery of questions that can be used throughout company interviews. This doesn't mean that your experience will always be good, but remember that the process is designed simply to find the right person for the role.

Many of the questions you'll be asked are predictable – so by thinking about your responses to these you should be well prepared and taking the first step to success. Remember that you have had interviews before. Learn from the past to prepare yourself for the future.

SUNDAY
MONDAY
TUESDAY
WEDNESDAY
THURSDAY
FRIDAY
SATURDAY

Fact-check (answers at the back)

There is more than one possible answer to some of the following questions.

1. What should your first thought be when you are invited to an interview?
   a) I hate interviews. ❏
   b) I hope I don't let myself down. ❏
   c) Great – they think I can do the job. ❏
   d) What will I wear? ❏

2. Interview experience is most like what?
   a) Performance appraisal ❏
   b) Office outings ❏
   c) Team meetings ❏
   d) Internal promotion ❏

3. What does an interviewer aim to find out?
   a) Whether you lived up to your CV ❏
   b) Information about your employer ❏
   c) Whether you seem nervous ❏
   d) If you are too good to be true ❏

4. What is the purpose of an interview?
   a) An opportunity to show off ❏
   b) An opportunity to learn about the organization ❏
   c) To be a two-way process ❏
   d) To trip you up ❏

5. What should your interview objective be?
   a) To present yourself well ❏
   b) To explore the benefits package ❏
   c) To meet your prospective colleagues and boss ❏
   d) To be clear about whether or not to accept the role ❏

6. How should you respond to a closed question?
   a) With a simple yes or no ❏
   b) By giving an example ❏
   c) With another question ❏
   d) With a nod and a smile ❏

7. What is the most important part of an interview?
   a) Warm-up questions ❏
   b) Questions about match and suitability ❏
   c) The end of the interview ❏
   d) Your questions ❏

8. What characterizes probing questions:
   a) They require detailed answers ❏
   b) They are unfair ❏
   c) They make you sweat ❏
   d) They indicate the interviewer's interest ❏

9. How should you respond to a discriminatory question?
   a) Get up and walk out ❏
   b) Clarify the interviewer's intention ❏
   c) Ask how it's relevant ❏
   d) Make a formal complaint ❏

10. How should you respond to an interviewer who hasn't read your CV?
    a) Allow them time to do so ❏
    b) Tell them all about it ❏
    c) Keep calm and be patient ❏
    d) Show irritation ❏

MONDAY

Doing your research

It is a natural human reaction to feel nervous and apprehensive going into an unfamiliar situation. Although elements of the interview will be unknown, there are, as we suggested yesterday, many features that interviews have in common. Interviewers will want to know about your previous experience, your personality and what makes you the ideal person for the post, or not. There are, however, aspects that are unique and unpredictable. No two experiences of being interviewed are likely to be the same. It is important, therefore, to gather as much information as you can at the earliest possible opportunity. This is easy to do and has the following benefits:

- You will demonstrate to the interviewer that you have considered the organization's requirements.
- You will show your interest in the job.
- You will feel more confident knowing that you are well prepared.

We suggest that you research three areas:

1 The interview
2 The job
3 The organization.

By researching, you lessen the risk of feeling that you could have made a better impression or that you haven't done yourself justice. The more you research, the greater knowledge and understanding you will gain. You will be better able to put yourself into the interviewer's shoes and have a sense of what it might be like to work with and for them. You will understand the company's acronyms and operating principles. In addition, you place yourself ahead of the competition.

The interview

If you have been invited for interview, you need to know some basic facts and, if this information isn't supplied, you need to start your investigations to find out:

● how to get there
● who will interview you
● the format of the interview.

How to get there

Finding out how you get to the interview is essential before you start your journey. Once you know the location, you can decide how you will travel. Always aim to arrive early – calculate the journey time and add an hour. Whatever method of transport you choose, delays may happen that are out of your control. Also check what security arrangements there are, as these may add time to your journey. On larger sites, leave yourself plenty of time to get from the reception to the interview building.

 If possible, go on a practice journey as it gives you the opportunity to view the site at close quarters without the interview looming.

On the day

If you are delayed, be sure to contact the interviewers and let them know why you will be late and when you expect to arrive. Make sure you have the relevant phone number handy. They will appreciate your call as they may need to make other plans or reschedule.

On arrival

Having arrived early, you will have the opportunity to make last-minute preparations:

● Think through your replies and questions.
● Get a feel for the organization.
● Complete any further application forms.
● Read through the company literature.
● Take advantage of other information.
● Go on a site tour.
● Read your CV again.
● Relax.

Who will interview you?

The key information you need here is: name(s), position in the organization and job title.

There may be a number of interviews, particularly for a senior post. The first, in-depth interview is often held on a one-to-one basis with a recruitment consultant, line manager or member of the human resources department. It could take the form of a thorough exploration of your CV or a structured interview.

Candidates shortlisted from the first interview can expect second and third interviews, which are likely to be conducted by one or more senior staff, who may have responsibility for the post or an interest in it. The objectives for these interviews are to explore any aspects still outstanding from the first interview and to assess how well your personality will blend with the team. You may meet the same interviewer more than once – so learn to pace yourself and aim to remember names.

Knowing who is going to interview you will help you prepare your responses. Interviewers' interests may fit into the categories described in the following table.

Organizational role	What they are looking for
Functional head	Qualifications/experience Ability to perform tasks Understanding of the job/technical jargon Transferable skills Match with management style, expectations and culture
Managing director	Ability to meet targets Contribution to growth and profitability Adaptability and aspirations
Peers	Teamworking, personality and style Shared experiences Work experience
Junior staff	Management style, openness Approachability
Human resources	Your background and career to date Training/development needs Salary and benefits Start date

Organizations employing recruitment consultants often use them to shortlist candidates to ensure that only the most qualified candidates progress. They will be seeking the person who most closely matches the employer's specification, not solely in terms of experience but also in personality and aspirations.

The format of the interview

Interviews can take many forms. The two most common are one-to-one and panel interviews. Some organizations combine different types by shortlisting candidates with a telephone interview, inviting them to a panel and then asking them to return for further one-to-one interviews. Once you have found out the format, you can gear your preparation specifically to suit.

Interview formats include:

- telephone
- one-to-one
- panel
- tests
- presentations
- socials.

Telephone

The informal pre-interview chat is often over the telephone. This may occur when the interviewer is uncertain whether to shortlist you. For you, this call could be very important, making the difference between winning a face-to-face meeting or not. Anticipate this by keeping a checklist by the phone.

One-to-one

This type of interview consists simply of one interviewer talking to one applicant. It is the easiest interview to arrange and conduct and, in consequence, is the type most commonly used.

However, decisions are rarely the result of one person's perceptions. It is common to hold a series of one-to-one interviews, which may be on the same day or extend over months.

Panel

The panel (or 'selection board') may number from two members upwards. It can take many different forms, from a free-for-all, where all interviewers chip in with a variety of questions, to a more formal and structured approach where interviewers will take it in turn to ask questions reflecting their particular interests. At first, this style of interview may feel more threatening, but it tends to be fairer and more equitable.

Panel interviews can be very formal. Responses and further exploratory questions are not always forthcoming because of the limitations of time. It is also more difficult to establish the same feeling of rapport as you can in a one-to-one interview.

The chair of the panel is usually the one who makes the initial introductions and the final remarks. Do not assume that they have the greatest influence in making final decisions.

Do not be unnerved by the panel; treat it as if it is a one-to-one interview, concentrating your attention on the person asking the question at all times. Only include the other members when you are ready to continue with the next question.

● Always look at the person asking the question.
● Direct your answer to the questioner.
● Glance around to show you are ready for the next question.

TIP *Do not be put off by signals between members of the panel. These probably have little to do with you personally but are more to do with matters such as time.*

Tests

Tests are now commonly used to help assess candidates' abilities, aptitudes and personality. They are not an examination of your ability to remember facts but an extra way of gathering information. All applicants will be given the same questions, tasks and parameters. In an assessment centre format these may be carried out in groups.

Test type	Measures
Aptitude	Specific skills for the job: verbal, numerical, spatial, mechanical, clerical
Psychometric	Personality traits and preferences which may be needed to fit into team/project, temperament, disposition
Attainment	Knowledge of procedures, skills: driving, typing, technical terminology
Intelligence	General intellectual potential, problem-solving skills

SUNDAY

MONDAY

TUESDAY

WEDNESDAY

THURSDAY

FRIDAY

SATURDAY

Test type	Measures
Physical	Health, eyesight, colour perception, hearing acuity
Group discussions	Communication, judgement, reasoning, problem solving, persuasiveness, listening skills, respect
Presentations	Ability to stand up and speak, arranging information, quick thinking, flexibility
Written exercises	Clarity, legibility, summarizing

If you know there will be some form of test, remember to complete it within the time allowed, read the questions and answer them honestly.

Presentations

It is increasingly common for interviews to require you to give a formal presentation as part of the process. You may get advance warning of this and the particular subject area you are required to present. Be sure to check what equipment will be available to you on the day (projector, laptop, software, flipchart, etc.) and who will constitute your audience. You may want copies of your presentation or a summary to hand out. Be creative and remember that you want your presentation to be memorable.

Occasionally you will receive a topic to present or a project to plan on arrival at the interview and have to prepare there and then. Think through an outline of a presentation – how and in what ways you would address the issues of the day. Then all you need to do if you are faced with this scenario is to adapt it to the specific requirements of the topic.

Your presentation should:

● convince the audience that you are qualified and experienced
● demonstrate successes
● outline your contributions on a strategic and detailed level
● establish good relationships.

Be sure to inject:

● professionalism
● a degree of formality

- controlled enthusiasm
- pace and drive
- humour, as long as it's natural.

Think how to make your presentation unique and interesting. Limit the number of PowerPoint slides you use to five per 20 minutes. Is there something you could take along as a prop that represents you or the organization in a memorable way? One candidate we know took a hat from a Christmas cracker and used it to demonstrate that they considered the interviewing company to be the king of kings in the sector. Corny, perhaps, but she was remembered with a smile and called back for the next interview.

A presentation is an ideal opportunity for you, but only if you can control your nerves and are clear about the messages you want to communicate. It is likely that this presentation will be related in some way to the job in question and most particularly to the main area of responsibility. Presentations can also be used to establish a relationship with the interviewer.

You should also consider whether it is appropriate to take a portfolio with you containing samples of your work. To be helpful, such things must be clearly relevant and easy to handle and look at during an interview.

Socials

Part of your interview day could include meeting the team or taking a tour of the organization. Some organizations arrange social gatherings where you, the other candidates and sometimes partners meet together with your future employers. These may be labelled informal events, but always be on your guard; they are a part of the interview process. Use this as another opportunity to gather information. Be sure to talk to all those representing the organization and limit your consumption of alcohol.

> *Investigating what will happen before the interview – who will interview you and the format of the interview – will help you to show your understanding of the role, the organization and current challenges, and also creates a more complete impression of whether the role fits with your career plan.*

The job

The essential starting point for success is to know as much as you can about the job for which you have applied. There are several potential sources of information; you should use as many as possible. These include:

● preliminary discussions
● personal contacts – your network
● the Internet.

Preliminary discussions

You will already have received some information about the job, which attracted you enough to make the initial contact. You may now want to know more about:

● the extent of your duties and responsibilities
● the desirable and essential qualities required
● skill levels and academic qualifications needed
● reporting relationships
● opportunities for training and development
● location
● hours of work
● salary and benefits.

Personal contacts

You may decide to collect information about the job by talking to someone involved in the recruitment process. If you remain unsure about any particular aspects of the job or the organization, you can save everyone's time by doing some research. This is your opportunity to check fit and suitability – yours and theirs.

● Does your network extend into the organization?
● Who do you know who works, or has worked, for them?

By talking to insiders, you can get an 'inside' view. Remember that you will be hearing a subjective perception. Their views may be affected by personal circumstances or prejudices. So concentrate on facts rather than opinions.

The Internet

You should be able to find plenty of information via the Internet, depending on the size and type of the organization. The challenge here is to avoid information overload and target your searches to particular areas of interest around the organization and to those relating to the post.

The organization

The interviewer will expect you to have some knowledge of the organization. It is unlikely that it will be either comprehensive or complete. You need to show your interest not only in what you know but in filling in the gaps.

If sufficient information is not already supplied, you should try to find out:

- what the organization does
- product details
- ownership (public, private, group, independent, UK)
- size
- history
- structure (site, area or department)
- management style
- culture
- staff turnover
- outlets/factories/offices
- turnover and profit
- market position
- stability
- reputation
- strengths
- weaknesses
- threats
- markets
- competitors.

The organization itself and, if it is large enough, its public relations or customer services departments, are excellent starting points.

Other potential sources of information include its website, the Internet, directories and databases.

Directories

Key British Enterprises – basic corporate data on Britain's top 50,000 companies. Includes full contact details, names and titles of executives, financial details and industry

Who Owns Whom includes parent companies, subsidiaries and associates

Kompass produces *Regional, Product and Service Directories* on over 40,000 leading companies. Includes contact names of directors, executives and department heads, nature of business, annual turnover www.kompass.com

Online databases

Company Searches: company information online
www.companysearches.co.uk

Avention, formerly Onesource: information on history, executive and finances
www.avention.com

These directories and databases are available from public and business libraries. More detailed information is available from Companies House.

Companies House
Crown Way
Cardiff CF14 3UZ
www.gov.uk/government/organisations/companies-house

Outside the UK, internationalcompanyinformation.com is a good source of data.

Use your networks, arrange to talk to your contacts and, if possible, borrow literature not normally given out to the public. Recruitment consultants are another good source of information; they should be able to help you access the formal information in the form of annual reports, sales literature and in-house magazines. They can also provide you with an insight into informal information: personalities, problems and opportunities. Use everything that is to hand.

It is more than likely that you will use the telephone for some of your enquiries. Be sure to have thought through and have listed in front of you the questions you propose to ask.

For example, you may want more details about:

- the job for which you are being interviewed
- who will interview you – their name and job title
- the format of the interview
- how long you will be there
- the name, address and phone number of the organization
- the name, address and phone number of the interview location
- the date, day and time of the interview
- the availability of car parking facilities
- security arrangements
- the name and title of the person arranging the interview
- the job location
- annual reports.

You may also want to ask about salary and benefits. It can save you time if you decide at this stage that you are no longer interested because the salary is too low. Proceed on this basis with caution, though, because salaries are often negotiable within parameters, but the person on the telephone may not be aware of these parameters and the level of flexibility.

These days you may be greeted by a message rather than a person. Consider and write down what you want to say before making the call. The key information you need to leave is:

- your name
- your contact telephone number
- your address
- a brief message, requesting information
- your deadline if you have one
- your availability.

Repeat your name and phone number at the end of your message.

You may be asked to put all questions into an email for a specific person's attention. Use the guidelines above and frame your email in a way that is not too formal and shows a degree of professionalism. Put yourself in the shoes of the email recipient, be clear which your most pressing questions are and be selective. If you haven't had a response within a week, you might try a reminder email or phone call – you are probably not as high a priority for them as they are for you!

All preparation is valuable, so invest time and energy into gathering as much information as you can at this stage.

Summary

Today we have guided you through the research you need to do to prepare for your interview.

To remove uncertainty and apprehension, investigate what will happen at the interview, including who will interview you and the format of the interview. Don't overlook the need to understand how to get to the interview and access the site; and always leave enough time to get there.

Today we've also encouraged you to research the role and the organization. We are sure that through your application you will have come to understand the role, and as you've been asked to interview you have the right skills and experience, so it's worth revisiting what you said in your application and all the information regarding the role.

If you have contacts within the department or organization, it's worth asking them for advice or further information. Do as much research as you can about the organization – both online and through your networks. Don't base your understanding only on reputation, however: look at current performance and challenges.

SUNDAY
MONDAY
TUESDAY
WEDNESDAY
THURSDAY
FRIDAY
SATURDAY

Fact-check (answers at the back)

There is more than one possible answer to some of the following questions.

1. Before an interview, what should you do?
   a) Always prepare thoroughly ❏
   b) Never prepare ❏
   c) Only prepare the presentation ❏
   d) Prepare just enough ❏

2. When planning how to get to an interview, what should you do?
   a) Look into transport ❏
   b) Leave enough time to get there ❏
   c) Check security arrangements ❏
   d) Assume there'll be parking ❏

3. Which person is most likely to interview you?
   a) Line manager ❏
   b) HR manager ❏
   c) Recruitment consultant ❏
   d) Any of the above ❏

4. How should you prepare for a telephone interview?
   a) They are informal so no need to prepare ❏
   b) Keep a checklist by the phone ❏
   c) Impossible to prepare for ❏
   d) By making yourself comfortable ❏

5. What can psychometric tests accurately gauge?
   a) Personality ❏
   b) Fit ❏
   c) Ability ❏
   d) How good your memory is ❏

6. When you are asked to do a test, what should you do?
   a) Put yourself in the shoes of the successful candidate ❏
   b) Answer as you think you should ❏
   c) Check that you have been consistent ❏
   d) Answer flippantly ❏

7. Presentations give you an opportunity to what?
   a) Shine ❏
   b) Trip yourself up ❏
   c) Show off the technology ❏
   d) Demonstrate your ability ❏

8. If asked to give a spontaneous presentation, what should you do?
   a) Feel dread ❏
   b) Freeze ❏
   c) See it as an opportunity to show your expertise ❏
   d) Enjoy it ❏

9. How should you research the job?
   a) Go to your network ❏
   b) Read the competencies document ❏
   c) Phone up for more information ❏
   d) Use your intuition ❏

10. Why should you research the organization?
    a) It gives the company view ❏
    b) It gives you a sense of the employer ❏
    c) It is useful whatever the outcome of the interview ❏
    d) It informs your questions ❏

TUESDAY

Discovering what differentiate you

Self-knowledge is an essential ingredient of your preparation for the interview.

We have already suggested that you research the interview format, the job and the organization so that you are better informed about the process and will know what to expect. A most important ingredient in this preparation is finding out about yourself, so that you feel comfortable in presenting yourself to the interviewer.

This idea may seem a little strange: after all, if you don't know yourself, who does?

Today we will help you to know yourself better through a process of reflection. We will give you areas to think about and guidance on these.

Today you will get to know more about:

- yourself as a person
- your skills
- your limitations
- your strengths
- your achievements
- the essence of you.

Complete all the exercises – be brave, and test them out on colleagues, friends and anyone else you trust.

You, the person

When managers are asked to describe themselves, they tend to talk about what they do rather than who they are. They think of themselves in terms of their title and describe themselves as such: Operations Manager, Human Resources Manager, Finance Manager or Project Manager. These are, on many occasions, sufficient descriptors and speak for themselves, but do not expect that this will be enough at an interview. You need to understand and describe what skills make you successful in your role and what strengths make you different.

Being invited to attend an interview suggests that you match the interviewer's specification; you are halfway to success.

However, it is unlikely that you will be the only person who looks good on paper. The interview is your opportunity to stand out and be noticed. You want to convince the interviewer that you can bring enhanced benefits to their organization as well as being able to do the job.

To be successful, you need to make an impression and be different. The interviewer may see many interviewees in the course of a day, so the ones they will remember are the ones who are distinctive, who have something interesting to say or who can make a unique contribution to the organization or department.

The key to presenting yourself is to consider and understand your uniqueness. Ask yourself the following questions:

● What have I got that makes me special?
● What makes me fit?
● What is my key message?

The answers may come easily or you may have to return to these questions at the end of today when you have a clearer understanding of you.

Your skills

The first step in building up a picture of yourself is to appraise your skills.

● What can you offer the organization?
● What are your skills?

These common interview questions, while apparently simple, require thought, preparation and a level of introspection and reflection. Your answer should not simply be a regurgitation of your CV, relating what you have done.

It is more about when and in what contexts you have performed well, and the skills and competencies, contacts, knowledge and attitude you have applied or acquired in the process. Try to answer this question honestly and spontaneously:

● What can I do?

How comfortable would you feel about presenting these ideas to an interviewer? It can feel strange at first to 'blow your own trumpet', but in an interview you are the only one who knows the tune.

The following list of national management standards is basically a set of 'can do' statements. Look down the list of skills in the table and give yourself a score for each statement against the following measures:

1 Very competent
2 Competent
3 Adequate for the task
4 Have not developed the skills

Check afterwards with a colleague to see if they agree with your assessment. You may find you have been overly critical.

People are generally less good at recognizing their own skills than at identifying skills in others. If you find you are struggling with this task, ask for feedback from the people you manage, or those who manage you; alternatively, think back over past appraisals and the feedback you have received.

Assess your skills

	1	2	3	4
Managing self and personal skills				
Manage your own resources	❏	❏	❏	❏
Manage your professional development	❏	❏	❏	❏
Develop your personal network	❏	❏	❏	❏
Providing direction				
Develop and implement operational plans for your area of responsibility	❏	❏	❏	❏
Map the environment in which your organization operates	❏	❏	❏	❏
Develop a strategic business plan for your organization	❏	❏	❏	❏
Put the strategic business plan into action	❏	❏	❏	❏
Provide leadership for your teams, in your area of responsibility and for your organization	❏	❏	❏	❏
Ensure compliance with legal, regulatory, ethical and social requirements	❏	❏	❏	❏
Develop the culture of your organization	❏	❏	❏	❏
Manage risk	❏	❏	❏	❏
Promote equality and diversity in your area of responsibility and in your organization	❏	❏	❏	❏
Facilitating change				
Encourage innovation in your team, in your area of responsibility and in your organization	❏	❏	❏	❏
Lead, plan and implement change	❏	❏	❏	❏
Working with people				
Develop productive working relationships with colleagues and stakeholders	❏	❏	❏	❏
Recruit, select and keep colleagues	❏	❏	❏	❏
Plan the workforce	❏	❏	❏	❏
Allocate and monitor the progress and quality of work in your area of responsibility	❏	❏	❏	❏
Provide learning opportunities for colleagues	❏	❏	❏	❏

Assess your skills

	1	2	3	4
Help team members address problems affecting their performance	❏	❏	❏	❏
Build and manage teams	❏	❏	❏	❏
Reduce and manage conflict in your team	❏	❏	❏	❏
Lead and participate in meetings	❏	❏	❏	❏
Support individuals to develop and maintain their performance	❏	❏	❏	❏
Initiate and follow disciplinary and grievance procedures	❏	❏	❏	❏
Manage redundancies in your area of responsibility	❏	❏	❏	❏
Build and sustain collaborative relationships with other organizations	❏	❏	❏	❏
Using resources				
Manage a budget	❏	❏	❏	❏
Manage finance for your area of responsibility	❏	❏	❏	❏
Obtain additional finance for the organization	❏	❏	❏	❏
Promote the use of technology within your organization	❏	❏	❏	❏
Identify, assess and control health and safety risks	❏	❏	❏	❏
Ensure health and safety requirements are met in your area of responsibility	❏	❏	❏	❏
Ensure an effective organizational approach to health and safety	❏	❏	❏	❏
Manage the physical resources	❏	❏	❏	❏
Manage the environmental impact of your work	❏	❏	❏	❏
Take effective decisions	❏	❏	❏	❏
Communicate information and knowledge	❏	❏	❏	❏
Manage knowledge in your area of responsibility and promote knowledge management in your organization	❏	❏	❏	❏

Assess your skills

	1	2	3	4
Support team and virtual working	❑	❑	❑	❑
Select suppliers through a tendering process	❑	❑	❑	❑
Outsource business processes	❑	❑	❑	❑
Achieving results				
Manage a project or a programme of complementary projects	❑	❑	❑	❑
Manage business processes	❑	❑	❑	❑
Develop and implement marketing plans for your area of responsibility	❑	❑	❑	❑
Develop a customer-focused organization	❑	❑	❑	❑
Monitor and solve customer service problems	❑	❑	❑	❑
Manage the achievement of customer satisfaction	❑	❑	❑	❑
Support customer service improvements	❑	❑	❑	❑
Work with others to improve customer service	❑	❑	❑	❑
Build your organization's understanding of its market and customers	❑	❑	❑	❑
Improve organizational performance	❑	❑	❑	❑
Manage quality systems	❑	❑	❑	❑
Prepare for, participate in and carry out quality audits	❑	❑	❑	❑
Manage the development and marketing of product/service in your area of responsibility	❑	❑	❑	❑

Reproduced with the kind permission of the
Management Standards Centre

This list may help to define your skills and give you the
language to talk about them. The next step is to own them.
Take some time now to tell yourself about your skills, and hear

SUNDAY MONDAY **TUESDAY** WEDNESDAY THURSDAY FRIDAY SATURDAY yourself saying them out loud without feeling embarrassed or apologetic. Practise in front of the mirror.

Your limitations

You are very likely to be asked about your weaknesses at the interview. We would prefer to think of them as limitations or areas for improvement and to look for positive ways of presenting them. For example, you know that you can be impatient, but looked at from an alternative perspective it could be seen as an over-eagerness to get things done. This is not hiding from the truth, it is putting an affirmative interpretation on negative characteristics.

Your 'weaknesses' can also be listed to give you an idea of what changes you might want to make.

- What limits you?
- What has held you back in your career?
- In what circumstances have you felt most frustrated and unhappy at work?

Your strengths

Skills are only part of the picture. They will help to show *what* you do. You have individual strengths which will dictate *how* you do things. This is what makes you unique.

The following list outlines the strengths of successful managers. Look at it and see where their talents coincide with yours. Mark yourself on a scale of 1–4:

1 Always
2 Frequently
3 Sometimes
4 Never

Where do your strengths lie?

	1	2	3	4
Quick thinking	❏	❏	❏	❏
Enthusiasm	❏	❏	❏	❏
Presence	❏	❏	❏	❏
Ability to handle conflict and make decisions	❏	❏	❏	❏
Self-confidence	❏	❏	❏	❏
Strength of will	❏	❏	❏	❏
Commitment and determination	❏	❏	❏	❏
Flexibility and willingness to change	❏	❏	❏	❏
Creativity	❏	❏	❏	❏
Willingness to take responsibility	❏	❏	❏	❏
Initiative	❏	❏	❏	❏
Competitiveness	❏	❏	❏	❏
Sensitivity to people and situation	❏	❏	❏	❏
Stamina	❏	❏	❏	❏
Commercial awareness	❏	❏	❏	❏
Judgement	❏	❏	❏	❏
Being personally organized	❏	❏	❏	❏
Ability to take risks	❏	❏	❏	❏
Ability to strike a balance between big picture and detail	❏	❏	❏	❏

You will notice that most of these qualities are not tested by any formal educational system. As a manager you can always learn the *skills* needed for the job. How many of the *strengths* listed can you learn?

Using this list for guidance, try to answer the following questions about your strengths. Be as specific as possible and think about descriptions of how you utilize them.

● What are the strong points of your character and personality?
● In so far as you have succeeded, what has helped you?

Understand your achievements

The most practical way to assess yourself is to make a list of all your achievements, not solely the major ones, but everything that other people should know about. People find this process difficult, so to help you we've given you some ideas. Add any more of your own.

Achievements might include:

- a new idea
- reducing waste
- turning around a bad situation
- avoiding potential problems
- improving customer relationships
- improving results
- costs you managed to cut
- an activity simplified or improved
- a crisis averted
- something you made
- a new skill mastered
- a group you led
- a problem solved
- anything that had a happy ending.

The essence of you

You have considered and listed your vast array of skills, strengths and achievements and examined your limitations. Now is the time to put them together to form a composite picture of you.

Write down a number of sentences beginning with the words 'I am', e.g. 'I am a manager.' Try to think of at least 15 of these.

Be specific

Expand these sentences to show yourself off. Add to the sentences by explaining and giving clear examples. Where possible, angle the examples to match the post for which you will be interviewed.

Produce statements such as:

I am a good manager because I am able to motivate and develop people. In my last job I inherited a team who were bored with the weekly meetings and often strolled in late. I talked to them individually, found out their dissatisfactions and instigated a system of agenda setting that involved them all. As a result the meetings became fun and much more productive.

This is very different from saying: 'I am a good manager because I have an MBA' or, 'I am a good manager because I have worked for "X" for 20 years.'

You can see from this example that the way you describe yourself and the kind of language you use detracts from or adds to the image you portray.

As well as giving concrete illustrations, you also need to think about your language. Be confident and assertive, using phrases like the following to illustrate your point positively:

... which resulted in
... so that
... the benefit was
... the advantage was

Dismiss all your tentative language such as:

I probably could...
I think I can...
I have been told...
Some people think I'm...

Summary statement

You may like to reinforce your other statements by developing a summary career statement about yourself. This has the advantage of creating the right impression in the mind of the interviewer. Produce a powerful statement about the type of person you are and the contribution you can make to the organization. You are then able to create value in the eyes of potential employers and emphasize the benefits you bring.

Statements such as:

I am a successful sales manager with a proven track record of building teams and winning high profile.

I am a determined professional with experience across a wide range of technical products.

These statements should be brief and powerful, highlighting all the benefits of employing you. Be sure to practise saying them out loud; often statements that look good on paper do not translate to the spoken word naturally. After hearing it you may need to adapt it. Also, be sure that you feel comfortable with the statement; if there is any hint of uneasiness, this will show.

Try it out before the interview and validate your perceptions against another reliable source. Use a friend or work colleague who knows you well. Looking at yourself through different people's eyes can demonstrate the different facets of you. Begin by trying to share your findings with a trusted friend or colleague. Ask them what skills they think you have. Ask them in what areas they feel you should be developing. Ask them to comment on your transferable skills.

Self-esteem

Self-esteem is essential to everyone's wellbeing and it is something that can grow or diminish depending on what is happening in our lives.

It can be divided into two parts:

- **Internal self-esteem** comes from your beliefs about yourself, accepting your strengths and limitations rather than striving to be perfect. You see yourself as equal to but different from other people rather than superior or inferior.
- **External self-esteem** comes from interactions with others. You respond to their reactions, opinions and how they relate to you. You let them tell you how good you are.

Many people have an over-developed need for external self-esteem because their internal self-esteem is fragile. As you increase your internal self-esteem, you will lose some of your dependence on external self-esteem.

You may find you spend time rating yourself as better in some areas and worse in others. Internal self-esteem is not dependent on comparisons. It is your own assessment of your self-worth. What you have developed today is a collection of ideas that reflect your strengths and achievements.

Summary

Modesty or traditional conditioning may have made today challenging, but it's better that the challenge comes in your preparation than at the interview. You need to be able to describe you – what makes you different and fit with the role. Using the organization's language can help, as can yesterday's research.

The interviewer wants to know what you offer and the difference you would bring to the role – your skills, strengths and achievements. This is always difficult to communicate on paper, so today was about bringing your CV or application to life. Now is not the time to be a shrinking violet. Let them know confidently and clearly how good you are.

It may help to approach the interview as you would a product launch. At the interview, you are the product; your challenge is to convince the other parties to invest in it. This will help you overcome any nervousness about 'bragging' because you will be one step removed from selling yourself.

Your journey to succeeding at interview is well on its way – you have done your research and prepared responses to questions. Tomorrow will be more about how you present yourself.

SUNDAY

MONDAY

TUESDAY

WEDNESDAY

THURSDAY

FRIDAY

SATURDAY

Fact-check (answers at the back)

There is more than one possible answer to some of the following questions.

1. How should you describe yourself?
a) Use your job title ❏
b) Say what you look like ❏
c) Detail your skills ❏
d) Feel embarrassed ❏

2. When you describe your skills, what should you talk about?
a) Your CV ❏
b) Your successes ❏
c) What makes you different ❏
d) How you've made a difference ❏

3. How should you respond to questions about your skills?
a) Struggle to find the words ❏
b) Use your organization's competencies ❏
c) Refer to what you've done ❏
d) Describe value you've added ❏

4. How would you prepare for questions about who you are?
a) Talk to your boss ❏
b) Talk to a colleague ❏
c) Look back over appraisals ❏
d) Fail to prepare ❏

5. How should you answer questions on your weaknesses?
a) By covering them up ❏
b) By presenting your strengths ❏
c) With embarrassment ❏
d) By saying what you learned from them ❏

6. How should you describe your strengths ?
a) As the way you do things ❏
b) What you do ❏
c) Your unique contribution ❏
d) The things that have helped you succeed ❏

7. Which of your achievements would be best to include?
a) Turning around a situation ❏
b) Improving results ❏
c) Acquiring new skills ❏
d) Surviving interviews ❏

8. What should 'I am' statements be?
a) Backed up by examples ❏
b) Clear ❏
c) Listed alphabetically ❏
d) Funny ❏

9. What do you demonstrate your strengths in terms of?
a) Your successes ❏
b) Your academic achievements ❏
c) All the jobs you've done ❏
d) Previous feedback ❏

10. How should you prepare for questions about yourself?
a) Practise with a colleague ❏
b) Practise being modest ❏
c) Practise feeling confident ❏
d) By using tentative, vague language ❏

WEDNESDAY

Preparing yourself for success

Some people see interviews as threatening situations. They worry about what limits them, about how nervous they get, about what the interviewers will think of them, and about failing to do the job if they were appointed.

For these people, what stands in the way of conveying self-confidence is their overriding fear of failing themselves and their expectations. Their fear of failure overcomes their aspiration to succeed. In some, it can have a paralysing effect and completely ruin the interview.

If this is a description of you, then you need to begin thinking of yourself and your approach to interviews in a more positive light. You started the process yesterday thinking about your strengths and limitations; today we will help you to look and act the part too.

Prepare to succeed by:

- thinking positively
- making a good impression
- looking prepared.

Thinking positively

World-class athletes, among others, will confirm the importance of mental attitude to achieving the best performance. To give yourself the best possible chance at interview you will need to think yourself into a fully positive frame of mind. How you set about this will be a personal matter. But concentration on your strengths, and the certainty that you have the internal resources to cope with any difficulties, will go a long way.

Some people find it helpful to relax quietly and picture their success, both at the interview and in the subsequent post. They imagine this in great and vivid detail, visualizing the thoughts and sensations this will bring. Others treat themselves to something new, ensuring that they feel good inside and out.

However you go about this, it is in many ways the most crucial phase of the whole process of preparation. You need an inner conviction that you are important to yourself. If you do not feel a sense of your own wellbeing and self-worth, how can you convince others that you will be an asset to their organization? You have to think positively before you can act positively.

'Whether you think you can or you can't,
you're probably right.'

Henry Ford

Compare:

Thoughts –	'I'm sure they just asked me to make up the numbers. The others are bound to be better.'
Feelings –	Hopeless, inadequate, apprehensive
Outcome –	Poor impression, no conviction, unsuccessful interview

with:

Thoughts –	'They've picked me from all the applicants. I must stand a very good chance.'
Feelings –	Calm, confident, positive anticipation
Outcome –	Assured impression, mutual fact-finding, beneficial interview

Aim to direct your energy away from worrying about the interview and towards effectively preparing for it. Consider it as an opportunity, where you are both interviewing each other, not as a one-sided test. Most importantly, remember that, of all the people who applied, they have chosen you to interview.

If you are not nervous about attending interviews, then you should have little problem in this respect. But try to monitor whether you may be seen as overconfident and not taking things as seriously as you should. It is common for interviewers to mistakenly confuse confidence with arrogance.

To be just a little anxious, a little apprehensive, is good; it is generally facilitative rather than inhibitive. Only when you become very anxious do you begin to harm your prospects.

Making a good impression

People make up their minds about us in minutes. Never ignore this fact, particularly at an interview when you have a relatively limited time to make an impression.

Your initial impact is vital. You don't get a second chance to make a first impression, so make sure you:

- start well
- pay attention to your appearance
- are aware of your body language
- use your voice skilfully.

Start well

Whenever two people meet for the first time, they automatically start by evaluating each other on the basis of the non-verbal cues they receive. You and your interviewer will be doing just that as soon as you meet, whether in the interview room or on the walk from reception. It is a subconscious 'weighing up' time.

The interviewer will often base their judgement on this initial impression and spend the remainder of the interview looking to reinforce their view. You may be judged by nothing more than how you walk across the room, the strength of your handshake, or when and how you sit.

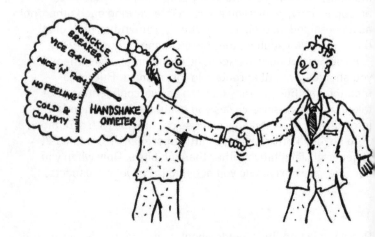

Evidence is often sought to support an initial impression. You should therefore do all you can to enter confidently, but not brashly, with a pleasant smile.

Do:

✔ Close the door behind you.

✔ Walk forward confidently; body straight, head up.

✔ Respond to offered handshakes firmly.

✔ Wait until you are invited to sit.

✔ Remain quiet but alert to the opening moves of the interviewer.

✔ Allow them to take the initiative.

✔ Be ready to respond appropriately.

Don't:

✗ Shuffle in, head down and hands in pockets.

✗ Carry a jumble of paper.

✗ Crash into the room pushing out your extended hand.

✗ Attempt to dominate an interview, especially in the opening stages.

Dress the part

It is essential that you dress the part. Your appearance reveals a great deal about your self-image, your values and your attitudes towards other people and situations. More favourable qualities are often attributed to smartly dressed people. Those who are perceived to be attractive and well groomed are often treated better than those considered unattractive or inappropriately dressed.

TIP *Beware of the danger of overdressing. A good benchmark is to decide how the holder of the job would be expected to dress, and go just one stage better.*

For interviews, it is wise to find out the dominant style or accepted image of the culture you are trying to enter. If you can visit the organization at lunchtime or the end of the day, go and see what people are wearing. If that is not possible, take a look at the organization's literature and website, which may contain photographs of employees and directors.

If you buy a special interview outfit, accessories or shoes, do ensure that they are comfortable. There can be nothing more distracting than shoes that pinch, a jacket too long in the arms, a material that creases, trousers too long or generally ill-fitting clothes.

Also be conscious of colours. More sober colours are often recommended for interviews: blues, blacks, greys with contrasting shirts and blouses. Your choice of tie, shirt, blouse or scarf is also important; any extremes of colour or pattern will make an impact. Think about the messages your appearance conveys to others.

Pay attention to the finer points of turnout: fingernails, hair, shoes and jewellery. Avoid too much perfume or aftershave. They won't be noticed if they are acceptable – but they will if they are not.

 Avoid drinking alcohol, smoking or eating highly spiced food just before an interview. Eat mints or use a breath freshener before; be cautious.

Use the right body language

You can communicate far more non-verbally than you may be aware. Although you often concentrate on what you are going to say – and it is important for self-confidence to do so – this must not be at the expense of how you say it.

Research shows that when you are presenting:

- words account for 35 per cent of the message
- tone of voice and body language account for 65 per cent of the message.

Negative thoughts and tension trigger anxious feelings. It is possible to overcome these – think about the directives 'chin up', 'stiff upper lip' and 'swallow your feelings' – using your body to control them. Beware of different messages through your body that can leak out and undermine or contradict what you are saying. If you are thinking positively about yourself and the interview, then your body will give a positive impression too.

Focus your attention on the interviewer to the exclusion of everything else. Ensure that you are comfortable and relaxed in the chair provided.

 Don't forget to listen carefully.

While listening and giving the interviewer your full attention, it is also important that you demonstrate this.

Do:

- ✔ Sit comfortably, in an upright but relaxed posture.
- ✔ Rest your hands on the arms of the chair or comfortably in your lap.
- ✔ Look at your interviewer with an interested expression.
- ✔ Keep your head raised when you listen.
- ✔ Nod intelligently whenever the interviewer tells you something
- ✔ Be relaxed.

Listed below are some of the most common blunders that interviewees make. They are things to avoid. In some way, these all suggest a desire to escape, boredom, nerves, or impatience either to speak or to leave.

Don't:

- ✗ Fidget or bite your nails.
- ✗ Cross your arms or legs, or clasp the chair or your upper arms.
- ✗ Lean backwards, looking away from the interviewer.

- ✗ Gaze fixedly at some point in the room.
- ✗ Become distracted by the carpet or a picture.
- ✗ Point your body towards the door.
- ✗ Kick or tap your foot.
- ✗ Tap a pen.
- ✗ Prop your head on the palm of your hand.
- ✗ Yawn.
- ✗ Stare blankly at the interviewer.
- ✗ Scribble on paper.

Use your voice skilfully

Your voice is crucial to the impression you make. Many people are self-conscious about their voices and accents and, fearing they will let them down, try to mask them. Often all this does is make them unintelligible. Your voice is unique and is part of what makes you who you are. So befriend it and, rather than trying to hide your accent, concentrate on being heard and understood. If you use your voice skilfully, you will sound confident, knowledgeable and enthusiastic.

Always speak in a clear, steady voice. If you hesitate or stumble you will appear nervous and ill prepared. If you are concerned about your voice, take care not to attempt to hide it. You will appear tense and closed up. Speak in your natural voice. Don't try to change it to impress the interviewer. Avoid bad language, slang, or annoying phrases or words such as 'you know' and 'actually', 'with respect' and 'to be honest'. Inject confidence, happiness and enthusiasm into your voice.

 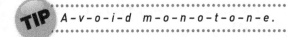

TIP

A – v – o – i – d   m – o – n – o – t – o – n – e.

Listen to your voice and get used to it. Take one of your statements from yesterday and record it. Say it as though you're very nervous or unsure. Try it in an angry voice or a suspicious one. Express it as if you feel proud and positive about it and you. Say it with a frown and a smile. Vary the words you emphasize and the way you say them. See how different you can make your voice sound and notice the effect on you of the different ways of saying it.

Do:

✔ Pause and breathe deeply before speaking.

✔ Speak slightly more slowly than normal.

✔ Speak clearly; open your mouth.

✔ Vary the tone to add interest.

✔ Relax your shoulders and jaw.

Don't:

✗ Rattle out words 16 to the dozen.

✗ Mumble.

✗ Cover your mouth as you speak.

✗ Stiffen your jaw.

✗ Talk to your shoes.

✗ Forget to breathe.

TIP

Own your responses: when talking about yourself, be sure to use the personal pronoun, 'I'. Identify with your responses, making sure they are specific to you.

Looking prepared

You may want to consider taking a folder with you. It is useful to hold your prompt notes, statements or questions. If not overused, this will give an air of efficiency. It can also help to reduce your nervousness and remind you of the two-way nature of the process.

Look and sound positive. Talk in a positive manner. If you're asked, 'Can you do this job?', the answer must never be, 'I think so' ' or, 'I hope so'. It should be, 'Yes, definitely.'

Be calm. Don't be distracted by interruptions. If the telephone rings or an interviewer's colleague enters the room, stay calm. Don't panic if you don't know the answer to a question. If you don't know, admit it. Also, if your mind goes blank, don't worry. Take a deep breath and ask for clarification. You can also repeat the question back to give yourself thinking time, but only do this once or twice, otherwise it can become a pattern and no one will listen to the answer that follows.

How you feel is essential to the impression you create. Use today as a practice.

Summary

You have got an interview and that means that the interviewer believes you could do the job, but there may be others who could do it too – so you have to shine. Your success is all about convincing the interviewer, but you may have to convince yourself first. You need to present yourself in a positive light, building on your skills, knowledge and achievements and, after today, you should be feeling more positive about that.

We saw today that the impression you make is much more about your presence than simply how you look. It's about everything from the moment you enter the room, greet people and take your seat. You can make a good impression with the tone and pitch of your voice and the energy you put into your responses – so don't allow your body language to let you down.

Don't overlook the need to listen attentively. Looking at the questioner can help, and they could be giving away clues too. Try to relax and not let nerves get the better of you, knowing that you have done your best to prepare.

SUNDAY
MONDAY
TUESDAY
WEDNESDAY
THURSDAY
FRIDAY
SATURDAY

Fact-check (answers at the back)

There is more than one possible answer to some of the following questions.

1. When approaching the interview, what should you focus on?
   a) Controlling your nerves ❏
   b) Not being able to do the job ❏
   c) What may go wrong ❏
   d) Your success in getting to this stage ❏

2. When preparing for the interview, what should you do?
   a) Think of yourself in the role ❏
   b) Relax ❏
   c) Find it difficult to overcome your negative thoughts ❏
   d) Not bother – you know you'll be all right on the day ❏

3. What's the best way to overcome interview nerves?
   a) Thorough preparation ❏
   b) Spending hours choosing what to wear ❏
   c) Having a couple of drinks for 'Dutch courage' ❏
   d) Talk over the interviewer ❏

4. How should you use your voice during an interview?
   a) Speak faster than normal ❏
   b) Speak more slowly than normal ❏
   c) By relaxing your jaw ❏
   d) By stiffening your jaw ❏

5. To create a good impression, what should you do?
   a) Walk confidently ❏
   b) Allow the interviewer to take the initiative ❏
   c) Ask lots of questions ❏
   d) Wait until you're invited to sit down ❏

6. How should you dress for an interview?
   a) Always in a suit ❏
   b) As you'd be expected to dress for the role ❏
   c) Wearing whatever's clean ❏
   d) It depends on your mood ❏

7. Which of the following should you pay attention to before the interview?
   a) Shoes ❏
   b) Fingernails ❏
   c) Hair ❏
   d) All of the above ❏

8. In the interview room, what should you do?
   a) Get comfortable, whatever the environment ❏
   b) Look at the interviewer who is asking you the question ❏
   c) Suggest a change in the layout of the room ❏
   d) Nod appropriately to show you are listening ❏

9. Which of the following should you avoid?
   a) Tapping your foot ❏
   b) Becoming distracted by activity outside the room ❏
   c) Sitting comfortably ❏
   d) Nodding appropriately ❏

10. In interviews, which of the following should you try to do?
   a) Maintain good eye contact ❏
   b) Stay positive and calm ❏
   c) Look down when responding to questions ❏
   d) Shout your message loud and clear ❏

THURSDAY

Responding
skilfully

Your preparation for the interview is now well under way. Just like a student before an exam, you should be confident that you have completed your revision, and be eagerly awaiting the big day. Continuing with the imagery, it is now time to look back over past exam papers, examine the questions asked, and plan your answers.

As you would expect, an interview is full of questions. These tend to be the same for each applicant, providing the key points for comparison. We looked at types of questions on Sunday; today we will focus on their content and give you guidelines for responding.

It is possible to anticipate and prepare in advance for many of the questions you will be asked. Interview questions have common themes. These are likely to be:

- self-assessment
- work history and experience
- the organization
- the job, ambitions and motivation
- management style.

Thinking about questions

One of the main objectives of the interviewer is to build an impression of the interviewee not solely based on experience and history. Competency-based interviews demand that you present evidence of your past experience and achievements.

When interviewers are more interested in your characteristics and how you see yourself, they are likely to ask questions about:

● reasons for applying for the job
● creativity and problem solving
● adaptability and dealing with ambiguity
● reliability
● ability to delegate
● team player or solo worker
● motivations and aspirations.

Knowing yourself is essential. Completing the exercises on Tuesday will have helped you to formulate your answers.

Listed below are some of the questions frequently asked at interviews. Think through your answers and read through the guidelines on responding. It may help to note your thoughts down on paper. They can serve as an aide-memoire for you for the future and something to return to and improve on. You may want to record your answers and listen to them. If you do, practise putting the right enthusiasm and energy into them.

Consider how you portray yourself. You need to be sure that you can leave the interviewer with a positive impression. They need to be confident that you can do the job, fit with peers and contribute to the organization as a whole.

 Remember that your application has already impressed the organization and that is why they are interviewing you. The interview is all about bringing what's on paper to life, so everything you do or say should reflect your ability to do the job and deliver the expectations. If you just restate your experience, you'll be missing your best opportunity to sell yourself.

Self-assessment

These questions aim to see how you sell yourself and how well you communicate that to others. They are usually very open questions that leave the direction of the answer up to you.

Tell me about yourself.
Because this is often the opening question in an interview, be very careful that you don't talk too much. Keep your answer brief, covering topics such as early years, development, management style, significant events and people. Think about the type of job and organization; what are they looking for? Choose the bits of you that match best. Be selective; for example, the early highlights and your technical skills may be less relevant to a management role than your proven management skills.

What are your weak points?
Weaknesses can be the other side of strengths. Having prepared yourself, you can make sure that limitations sound like strengths, and give examples. Always admit to one (or, if hard pressed, a second) limitation; if you don't, it suggests you don't know yourself very well.

I can take longer than others to finish a task, unless there is a deadline to meet. My weakness is linked to a strength – being very thorough.

What are your strengths?
Focus these on the post applied for and again give concrete examples. After reading Tuesday's chapter you will have plenty of successes to relate. Sort through them before you go to your interview and make them relevant.

I can quickly create a harmonious atmosphere with new clients. They feel relaxed and we can talk business straight away.

What can you do for us that someone else can't?
Here you have every right to blow your own trumpet and sell yourself! Talk about your record of getting things done, give examples and be specific. Mention your skills and interests combined with your history of getting results.

This is your opportunity to illustrate your uniqueness and the benefits you can offer the organization. You need to create an image of yourself as someone who stands out as a greater potential asset than any of the other applicants.

Work history

This section of questions focuses on what you can draw from your practical work experiences. It may be that there is little that differentiates you from the other applicants on paper, so the spotlight is on the way you present your employment and its relevance to date.

If you could start your career again, what would you do differently?
After a brief review of options, come back to something very like your work so far. You may want to add something you would have changed earlier in your career rather than starting again. It is fine to be content; explain why you are happy as you are, rather than just saying you would change nothing.

Now I realize how much I enjoy being a manager, I would have put myself forward for a management position sooner.

I knew when I was at school that I wanted to be a chief accountant. I planned my education and job applications to this end.

Why are you leaving/did you leave your present position?

Beware of becoming defensive on this question. Prepare yourself well. If you are leaving your present position because of problems with people, problems in the marketplace or because of withdrawn finances, you need to consider your responses carefully. Look to future opportunities rather than past problems. After all, few decisions are the result of just one factor: they are usually due to a combination of circumstances.

Resist any temptation to criticize or blame other people for your problems. You need to be seen as taking some responsibility for what happens to you.

I believe everyone should manage their careers; I now recognize the limited opportunities for me within my current organization and am actively seeking a change.

In your current/last position, what features do/did you like the most? Which the least?

Be careful and positive. Try to enhance the picture of you that the interviewer already has. Be sure to describe many more features that you liked than disliked. When you mention any you disliked, describe ways in which you overcame them.

I believe in regular communications and I had to work hard to win my colleagues over to a similar belief; we now have systems in place for regular contact that I am proud of.

What were your most significant contributions in your last position?

Have specific examples ready. Link these wherever possible to the achievements you have on your CV and to the post in question. Ensure that these give a balanced impression of you. You may want to describe the contributions you made through managing and developing people, or to areas of organizational development.

Did you think of leaving your present position before? If so, what held you there?

What makes you stay in any particular job and what prompts you to start looking for other opportunities? It may be challenge, colleagues, culture, influence, etc. Ensure you communicate that you know what is important to you at work and that you take control when things don't appear to be going right.

Would you describe a few situations in which your work was criticized?

Be specific. Think about constructive criticism and times when you've asked for feedback. You may then want to relate this to changes you've made to the way you work.

I once lost my temper with a particular member of staff, but it helped me think about the way I give and receive feedback.

How do you react to pressure and deal with deadlines?

Observe that both are facets of your career and give examples from your experience in which you triumphed. You may also want to highlight what you have learned to help you deal with the pressure to ensure it doesn't exhibit itself as stress.

The organization

The interviewer will want to know how well you match their organization. You are both looking for a good fit: they want someone who will easily slot in and you want somewhere you will feel comfortable. All your research should prepare you well for these questions.

What do you know about our organization?
This question often precedes the interviewer's relating of a brief summary of the organization. Ideally, you should be able to discuss products or services, reputation, image, goals, problems, management style, people, history, philosophy. Your research from Monday will help you here. Let your response demonstrate that you have done the research, but don't overwhelm the listener. If you don't know much about the organization, it is better to say so than to pretend that you do.

Why do you want to work for us?
Relate this to the organization's needs. Your research may have shown that the organization is doing things you would like to be involved with. For example, if the organization is well known for a particular style of management, your answer should mention wanting to be a part of that. You should clearly identify what your contribution would be.

How long would it take you to make a meaningful contribution to our organization?
Be realistic. You may want to ask for further clarification on what the interviewer means by a meaningful contribution, or suggest what the most meaningful contribution could be in the short, medium and long term.

Use what you know about the organization and yourself

The interviewer is interested in how you will fit into the organization. Your research earlier in the week should help you think through how you display your personal and management style. Weave this into all your responses, so that if the organization is dynamic and evolving, with lots of ambiguity, use examples that reflect how you've managed in these environments previously.

But also think about the fit with you – if you enjoy the challenges that change brings but change is slow and there is resistance to it, you could be just what they are looking for but the role or organization may not be what you are seeking.

How long would you stay with us?
Be honest. While obviously interested in a career within their organization, you can outline what would encourage you to stay. This may be challenge, recognition, variety, etc. You may want to highlight your demonstrated loyalty and commitment to your current organization.

I expect to be a senior manager within five years and would be happy to achieve that within this organization.

What important trends do you see in our industry?
Be prepared with two or three. You may consider technology, economic conditions, political climate, responding to market demands or increased global competition. Be sure that you are up to date with your information. Read the relevant journals or visit websites as part of your preparation.

The job

This is the second part of the matching process. If you fit into the organization, do you have the requisite skills and personality to do the job?

What do you find most attractive about this position? What seems least attractive to you?
List three or four attractive features and one single unattractive one. Put a positive suggestion with the less attractive attribute.

I would like to look closely at the budgetary control system, as there seems to be scope for reorganization.

Why should we appoint you?
Be prepared for this as it is a common question. Be clear in your statements of your uniqueness and the ways in which you match their requirements regarding experience, strengths and characteristics.

What do you look for in a job?
Keep your answer oriented to the opportunity in question. You could focus on your desire to perform and be recognized for your contributions, or on your interest in working within that particular organizational environment.

I look for autonomy, which is clearly the way you expect your managers to work.

If you could do any job, what would it be?
It is hoped that your ideal is similar to the job you have applied for. Describe what an ideal job looks like to you in the context of the organization and culture. It should be evident from this why you have applied for the job. If not, then compare these ideals to the job you are applying for.

Management style

What is your management style?
Through your research you should know a little about the organization's styles of management. Find out about general management theory too. Be honest while demonstrating how your style will help you work within and make a contribution to the organization.

Are you a good manager? Can you give me some examples?
Keep your answer achievement and task oriented. Think about examples that demonstrate your success as a manager and the different aspects of this. Always talk of yourself in the present tense and in the first person, 'I am' rather than 'I have been told' or 'others say...'. The latter can sound as though you don't believe it.

Do you consider yourself a leader?
Even though this is a closed question, do not simply respond with a yes or no answer. Describe examples of leadership from your experience of leading a team, within your areas of responsibility and in the context of the organization.

What do you think is the most difficult thing about being a manager?
You could mention planning, implementation and budgets, although motivating, managing others and changing the culture are often cited as the most difficult tasks.

A word of warning

In responding to the interviewer's questions, there are also some areas to beware of.

Don't:

✗ Let the interview become an interrogation.
✗ Use weak evasive phrases: 'I have been told...'.
✗ Lie.
✗ Be a 'know it all'.
✗ Make jokes, especially against the interviewers.
✗ Speak ill of third parties.
✗ Blame others for what's gone wrong.

Do:

✔ Personalize your answers.
✔ Take responsibility for your limitations.
✔ Be genuinely interested in what they are saying.
✔ Be open to 'difficult' questions.

Summary

Today we have given you real examples of interview questions and answers. We have encouraged you to think about how you can leave the interviewer with a positive impression of you and your experience.

Remember that you are being interviewed because your application has already impressed the organization. The interview is all about bringing that life, so everything you do or say should reflect your ability to do the job and deliver the expectations. Don't just restate your experience and waste the opportunity to sell yourself.

The interviewer is also interested in how you might fit into the organization. Weave what you know about the organization from your research into all your responses. Think how you can best display your personal and management style. But remember that interviews are two-way: think about what you want and the fit with you.

So, have you answered these questions?

- Can you do the job?
- Will you do the job?
- Will you fit in?

SUNDAY
MONDAY
TUESDAY
WEDNESDAY
THURSDAY
FRIDAY
SATURDAY

Fact-check (answers at the back)

There is more than one possible answer to some of the following questions.

1. Which question types should you expect at interview?
a) Self-assessment and style ❑
b) Work history ❑
c) The role and the organization ❑
d) Personal life ❑

2. What impression should you give at interview?
a) One that reflects your performance ❑
b) One that is positive ❑
c) One that is negative ❑
d) One that overstates your ability ❑

3. When asked, 'Tell me about yourself', what should you do?
a) Tell your life story ❑
b) Focus on the role ❑
c) State what others have said about you ❑
d) Try to change the subject ❑

4. How should you answer the question 'What are your weak points?'
a) By presenting your strengths ❑
b) By saying you don't have any ❑
c) By admitting to all your weaknesses ❑
d) By taking the opportunity to display your self-knowledge ❑

5. How should you answer the question 'Why are you leaving?'
a) By becoming defensive ❑
b) By focusing on problems ❑
c) By discussing future opportunities ❑
d) By using a carefully rehearsed answer ❑

6. How should you describe your most significant contribution?
a) Talk about a specific achievement ❑
b) Relate it to the organization ❑
c) Say very little; you don't want to boast ❑
d) List your achievements ❑

7. What is the purpose of the question, 'How do you react to pressure?'
a) To encourage you to say how you've dealt with pressure ❑
b) To trick you ❑
c) To put you under pressure ❑
d) To lead you to describe learning throughout your career ❑

8. When answering questions about the organization, what should you describe?
a) Products and/or services ❑
b) The sector ❑
c) Challenges ❑
d) Your present organization ❑

9. If asked how long you would stay, how should you respond?
a) Honestly ❑
b) By outlining what would encourage you to stay ❑
c) By changing the subject ❑
d) By answering, 'As long as you'd have me.' ❑

10. How should you describe yourself?
a) In the first person, 'I am' ❑
b) By relating what others say ❑
c) With an air of disbelief ❑
d) As someone who 'knows it all' ❑

FRIDAY

Being proactive: asking questions

So far this week we have concentrated on the interviewee in a reactive role. Today, we will look at the interviewee from a different perspective, identifying opportunities to be proactive, to ask your own questions or to lead the discussion.

The interviewer needs to know that you can think for yourself and take the initiative. Choosing your questions is another important part of your preparation. You might want to prioritize them in order of importance in case you are limited by time. If you have rehearsed these questions, they will sound very natural as you ask them.

Your moves:

- Ask the right questions.
- Keep on listening.
- Express yourself effectively.
- End on a top note.

Ask the right questions

You will usually be given the opportunity to ask your questions towards the end of the interview. This is your chance to fill any gaps in your knowledge about the job and the organization and clarify the next step in the interview process. Even if they do not invite questions, you should make sure that you check whatever you need to know. Few things are worse than leaving an interview thinking, 'If only I had asked... !'

Good interviewers will offer plenty of chances for you to check your understanding about the post and the organization throughout the interview. It is still a good idea to have questions prepared that are based on your initial research and preparation. These may change or evolve as the interview develops.

The questions you ask will depend on how much information you have already collected, and your particular interests in the job. They should reflect your eagerness to work for the organization and show evidence of thorough research. The pattern we suggest relates back to the data you collected on Monday. Your questions may relate to:

● the job
● the organization
● the interview process.

Refer back to Sunday when thinking about the types of question to ask.

 Don't bombard the interviewer. Choose one or two critical questions only. And remember, you are still the interviewee, so watch you do not reverse roles. The interviewer does not want to be interrogated!

Work within the time left for the interview. If appropriate, check with the interviewer about time and ask no more than can reasonably be answered within that time frame. You can always ask, 'Who else should I be talking to?'

The job

Your questions about the job may fall into the following categories:

- Routine and difficult aspects of the work: day-to-day responsibilities, special projects.
- Full responsibilities of the job: reporting lines (up/down/ sideways), shared responsibilities.
- Support and guidance available to you: flexibility of budget, mentoring, coaching opportunities, bonus schemes, welfare.
- Amount of travel involved: relocation plans, other sites to visit.
- How often your performance will be reviewed: company appraisal scheme, performance reviews, are these pay/promotion related?
- Training and development opportunities: in-house schemes, qualifications, conferences.
- Promotion and career paths: company expectations, board appointments, directorships, senior appointments (internal/external).

Maintain the image you have portrayed throughout the interview. If you have focused on the fact that you are a team player, ask questions relating to the team. What are the interviewer's perceptions of its strengths and weaknesses? If you believe your performance will be a key factor in how you will be judged, ask about performance indicators or the organization's expectations over the next six months.

Questions to ask about the job

The following examples may help you formulate some questions of your own:

1 Why has the job become vacant?
2 What will you expect from me in the next six months?
3 What are the key tasks and responsibilities?
4 What is the biggest challenge facing this team at the moment?
5 What are the strengths and limitations within the team?

6 How do you review performance?
7 What development opportunities are there?
8 What would my future career prospects be?
9 Is promotion generally from within?

The organization

There may be some gaps in your knowledge about the organization. Keep your questions to areas that are not sufficiently covered in the information you have previously received during the interview.

Topics for questions about the organization may cover:

- Structure of the organization: hierarchical, flat, matrix, informal structure.
- Success of the organization: turnover, new products/services, domestic/international markets, financial health.
- Decision making: briefings, consultations, communications.
- Future strategy and long-term plans: mission, strategic plan, philosophy.
- Staffing: contraction, expansion, outsourcing.

These sorts of questions are essential to your decision making. Is this organization really viable in terms of profits and, if not, are funders, holding companies, bankers, etc., prepared to continue backing it for as long as it takes?

People have made bad decisions about jobs based on inaccurate information about the organization rather than based on their suitability and the attractiveness of the job. Continue your investigations after the interview if you are still interested. Research whatever sources are available; contact suppliers, customers, professional bodies, etc.

Questions to ask about the organization

The following examples of questions may help:

1 Could you clarify for me the structure of
  the organization?
2 How has the market been developing
  for products/services?
3 How are decisions made?
4 What problems do you envisage for the organization?
5 What plans are there for reorganization, expansion
  or retrenchment?
6 What are your strategies for growth?
7 How often do you update your business plan?
8 What is the annual staff/financial turnover?
9 How do you plan for succession throughout
  the company?

The interview process

You need to know what will happen once you have left the interview
room. The interviewer should already have told you at the start
of the interview, or the information may have been part of the
advertisement or your invitation to the interview. If you are still not
sure, ask. It is your right to have clarity about the procedure.

Questions to ask about the
interview process

The following example questions may help you:

1 When will I hear from you?
2 What is the next step: further interview,
  medical, tests?
3 How will I be informed: letter, phone call, email?

4 Is there further information you need from me?
5 Is there someone else I should see
  in the organization?

Your prepared questions will serve you well. Be sure to remember:

- Don't ask questions about information you have already been given.
- Don't ask questions for the sake of it.
- Do listen and ask supplementary questions.
- Do demonstrate that you have digested the information previously given.

Keep on listening

Throughout this book we have referred to the importance of listening to and understanding what the interviewer is saying to you or asking. We believe it is equally important to keep on listening when you are asking the questions. As the interview progresses and your time to ask questions approaches, be careful not to lose concentration. Many of the worst mistakes at interviews arise from candidates who fail to hear or understand the questions. If you're not sure what the interviewer means, ask for clarification; it doesn't mean you're stupid! In fact, just the opposite.

Too often, interviewees are in such a hurry to speak – usually out of nervousness, sometimes out of overconfidence – that they do not fully hear what has been said.

There is also the danger that you hear what you expect to hear rather than what is actually being said. Avoid preconceptions; let the interviewer answer your questions fully rather than prejudge the outcome or response.

Aids to listening

1 Give the other person your full attention; don't fidget.

2 Wait for them to finish what they are saying; don't interrupt.

3 Ask open questions for more information.

4 Regularly check your understanding; don't make assumptions.

5 Pay attention to your body language.

6 Be open-minded, not prejudiced.

Express yourself effectively

You want to present yourself in the best possible light throughout the interview process. This will involve effective answering of the questions asked, but also grasping any other opportunities to make your case. You should:

- Keep to the point.
- Be clear.
- Know the appropriate jargon.
- Speak with confidence.
- Keep your answers positive.
- Be honest and open with replies.
- Give plenty of concrete work-related examples.
- Be enthusiastic.
- Weigh up the interviewer.

Keep to the point

It is essential that you keep your questions and answers brief. In a short interview, aim to take no longer than two minutes with each. Only address the questions you have been asked and ensure your answers are relevant.

Structure your statements to ensure that your message is clear. You can achieve this in a number of ways. To make the most impact, limit your reply to one subject at a time; the more you try to include in your answer, the less the interviewer will get from it. So take time to think about which subject is most relevant to the job, the organization or the interviewer.

Be clear

Clarity in reasoning and expression is a skill which can be developed. Your aim should be to present your responses in an interesting and intelligible way, so that the interviewers are not left confused or uncertain. Be specific and talk about examples; always ask for precise details.

Know the appropriate jargon

Be careful not to talk in technical, functional or organizational shorthand that may lose the interviewer. We tend to assume the same knowledge base as those to whom we talk. At an interview this can be dangerous.

However, you should be familiar with any jargon connected with the job or the industry so that the interviewer doesn't leave you behind.

Speak with confidence

Be confident in all that you present. If you are not confident it will show. Let your body language reinforce your words. Be natural; let the interviewer see and appreciate the real you.

Be enthusiastic

Enthusiasm is a wonderful quality; it is a combination of energy and determination. Enthusiastic people are those who enjoy what they are doing and convey this to others. They are free from self-consciousness and are more in control of themselves.

Weigh up the interviewer

To succeed, an interview must be a two-way process. The interviewer will be trying (whether consciously or unconsciously) to find out how good the 'chemistry' or the rapport is likely to be. You should do the same from your side; few jobs are worth having if you are unable to get on with your boss. You should be alert for indications of honesty, efficiency, friendliness and the other characteristics you want from your manager.

End on a top note

There is a danger of relaxing too soon when the interview appears to be over and the interviewer is conducting you to the door. Fix in your mind the picture of yourself that you want the interviewer to keep and maintain, if you want to be sure that those last impressions are favourable. You should leave the interview room as you arrived, confidently but not brashly, shaking hands firmly and with a smile.

Do not assume the interview has ended until the interviewer makes it clear that it has.

If you are still interested in the job, a short letter to the person you met is invaluable. Handwritten notes are no longer commonplace and will be much appreciated. They show that you have taken some time and trouble rather than quickly sending off an email. You can thank them for the time they took to tell you about the job and the organization. Remind them of the key benefit you would bring to the company and briefly restate your reasons for wanting to work there.

Summary

So far this week we've encouraged you to prepare so you can respond skilfully. Today we have encouraged you to think about your moves and how you can be spontaneous but in control at the interview.

We've focused on preparing and asking the right questions. Interviewers are always impressed by good questions, which demonstrate that you've thought about the role in some detail. Do beware of going into too much detail, though, as this can come at the next stage.

Also think about the impression you want to create – once you have this fixed in your mind it's much easier to bring it to life.

Always remember:

● Maintain eye contact.
● Take your leave smoothly and politely.
● Do not add any afterthoughts.
● Shake the interviewer's hand.
● Thank them for giving you their time.
● Send a follow-up letter.

Tomorrow we will look at putting your research and preparation together – focusing you on success.

SUNDAY
MONDAY
TUESDAY
WEDNESDAY
THURSDAY
FRIDAY
SATURDAY

Fact-check (answers at the back)

There is more than one possible answer to some of the following questions.

1. What is the purpose of your questions at interview?
a) To fill gaps in your knowledge ❑
b) To clarify the next steps ❑
c) To fill in time at the end ❑
d) To show that you want the job ❑

2. How many questions should you prepare?
a) One or two ❑
b) At least ten in case you need to play for time ❑
c) Plenty, so that you can choose a few as appropriate ❑
d) None – you expect all points to be answered already ❑

3. What should your questions about the role relate to?
a) Day-to-day responsibilities ❑
b) How your performance will be measured ❑
c) Opportunities for socializing ❑
d) Who you should beware of ❑

4. What should your questions about the organization relate to?
a) Strategic plans ❑
b) Lunch and games facilities ❑
c) The competition ❑
d) Benefits ❑

5. How should you research the organization?
a) Through professional bodies ❑
b) Online ❑
c) Through the annual report ❑
d) Through the information you are sent ❑

6. When exploring what will happen next in the interview process, what should you ask?
a) 'When will I hear from you?' ❑
b) 'What is the next step?' ❑
c) 'Is there any further information you need from me?' ❑
d) 'I've had many offers, so can you let me know today?' ❑

7. If you didn't understand a question, what should you do?
a) Ask for clarification ❑
b) Answer with what you thought was meant ❑
c) Look puzzled ❑
d) Shrug your shoulders ❑

8. When do you express yourself best?
a) When feeling confident ❑
b) When feeling nervous ❑
c) When giving examples ❑
d) When talking a lot. ❑

9. How can you ensure your message is clear?
a) By limiting your responses to a maximum of two points ❏
b) By repeating it several times ❏
c) By its impact ❏
d) By getting across not only answers to the questions but all the other things you've prepared ❏

10. What kind of impression should you try to leave?
a) That you are the person for the job ❏
b) That you are confident ❏
c) That you are about to be snapped up elsewhere ❏
d) That you are better than the next candidate. ❏

SUNDAY

MONDAY

TUESDAY

WEDNESDAY

THURSDAY

FRIDAY

SATURDAY

SATURDAY

Putting it all together

We have come to the end of the week and your preparations are nearly complete. By this stage you should be feeling more confident about presenting yourself in the interview. An interview is, after all, your chance to shine.

Throughout the week we have focused on areas such as what to say, how to say it and what to do. Today we will aim to bring it all together. When you first learn a skill or technique such as driving, using new software or chairing meetings, you are anything but natural. But, with practice, these skills become natural extensions of you. Interviewing skills are no different. By following the steps from Sunday to Friday you will have developed your own interviewing style and many of your answers will seem almost instinctive.

Today we will focus on removing all the blocks that prevent you from being yourself. After all, your unique selling point is you. We will consider:

- objectives
- rehearsal
- readiness
- review
- feedback.

Objectives

As we discussed on Sunday, interviewers will have set their objectives before the interview and will have planned how these will be achieved. An interviewer's key objective is to find the right person for the job. Other objectives will reflect the stage of the interview; for example, in the final stages there will be greater emphasis on fit and characteristics rather than skills.

As an interviewee, you should also set objectives. Your main objective is to be offered the job. However, there will be secondary objectives ranging from presenting yourself in a positive light and exploring the real culture of the organization, through to deciding whether or not, as a result of the interview, you want the job.

These objectives should help you become more focused in preparing for the interview and clearer in the messages you want to communicate. This will help you make the right impression as the ideal candidate for the job, rather than just another runner.

Rehearsal

Most of us have never been taught to be interviewed. If you are lucky, you may have attended a workshop on the subject or received some feedback on how you presented yourself. It is more likely that the only experience you have had of interviews has been the real thing, for real jobs. You don't have the time to experiment; only poor performers get lots of interview practice. So you need to rehearse:

● your entrance
● your body language
● your voice
● your answers to questions
● the benefits you bring
● asking your questions
● taking feedback.

Don't let the success of your future depend on finding out how you interview on the day. Take time to practise. Practice develops performance in most things; interviews are no exception.

Ask a colleague, your partner, anyone whose opinion you value or trust, to act as the interviewer, then role-play the situation and take feedback. Before you participate in the 'interview' with them, show them your objectives, the job description and a prepared list of the kinds of questions you expect to be asked. Encourage them to ask their own questions too. Then you can see how you handle the unexpected.

It's a good idea to record your interview practice; you will learn more this way and much of it will be positive learning.

The better the rehearsal, the better the performance. Actors spend many hours rehearsing so that they are word perfect on the opening night. Remember, this is a performance of sorts and needs thorough preparation.

Your entrance

Have the person in the role of interviewer meet you and invite you to sit down. Don't tell them the image you want to create; check their perception later. Even at rehearsal it is quite likely you will feel nervous. This is fine; you will feel less anxious on the day as a result.

Your body language

We would encourage you to breathe deeply and relax in your own way. Sit upright in a comfortable position and look attentive. You are likely to be attentive if your body is. If you appear uneasy, the 'interviewer' will pick up on this through your body language and may not hear your excellent responses.

By rehearsing, you can find out whether you have any nervous and distracting mannerisms to change.

Your voice

Can the 'interviewer' hear you clearly? Do you sound convincing and interesting? To which questions do you give the most energetic answers? This can give you an idea of where your key interests lie. Listen to the rhythm in your voice; work at not being monotone. Be sure you have warmed up your voice before the interview starts. On the day you can go through some tongue twisters and vocal stretches as you travel to the interview.

Answers to questions

Experiment with the time you take to answer the questions. Just how long are the silences between the questions and your responses? Make sure to listen right to the end of the question and make your reply clear and specific. Resist the temptation to try to show how in tune you are with the 'interviewer' by jumping in with an answer before you have heard the complete question.

The benefits you bring

It is important to reassure the 'interviewer' throughout the interview that you are the person they seek. Introduce examples and case studies that reinforce your positive statements. Remember to turn any weaknesses into strengths and learning points. Illustrate how you can make a difference and bring something new and exciting to the organization.

Asking your questions

You will have some questions you prepared earlier; use the rehearsal to practise asking unprepared questions too. How clear and thoughtful are they? Be sure to keep them specifically related to that job or organization.

Feedback

After the rehearsal, make sure you have plenty of time to play back and discuss what happened. Listen carefully.

What can you improve? Also accept where you are strong, and feel confident about it. Recognize what you do well and ensure that you do more of it. Keep practising if you can. Draw up a checklist of the things you wish to rehearse and ask your 'interviewer' for comments and suggestions.

Readiness

Here are a few questions you might want to ask yourself just before you go to the interview:

- Am I ready?
- Are my clothes and shoes clean, neat and tidy?
- Is my hair tidy?
- Am I clear what image I want to project?
- Have I decided how to project that image?
- Have I warmed up and relaxed my voice?
- Can I be heard clearly?
- Am I walking/standing/sitting tall?
- Am I relaxed?
- Do I feel confident to answer the questions?
- Have I structured my answers for the best impact?
- Have I prepared a sheet of prompts/questions?

Review

By analysing and reviewing your performance after the 'real' interview, you can see where you might need to improve and so develop the necessary skills. It will help you to identify areas you need to strengthen if you are attending any more interviews. Be honest with yourself and acknowledge where you did well. Don't get into the post-exam habit of focusing on any questions you answered incorrectly and punishing yourself for so doing.

 Review your performance as soon as possible after the interview.

Remember that one of the most important questions to ask yourself is the one which began the week. Answer this honestly: 'Did I present myself in the best possible light?' The following checklist will help you to review your interview performance in more detail.

Did I:	✔
• arrive on time?	
• speak confidently to everyone I met?	
• handle the opening moments well?	
• feel and look relaxed?	
• maintain appropriate eye contact?	
• use the full range of my voice to convey my message?	
• stay cool and calm?	
• answer all the questions well?	
• expand my answers?	
• refer to my strengths?	
• listen carefully to the questions?	
• understand the questions before I replied?	
• work out in advance the points I wanted to make?	
• volunteer information when given the chance?	
• capture and hold the interviewer's attention?	
• impress the interviewer?	
• demonstrate my knowledge of the job and the organization?	
• ask good questions?	
• adapt and adjust my questions?	
• deal well with the closing moments?	
• end on a confident and optimistic note?	

These questions will give you an idea of what you need to focus on. If your answer is 'no' to any of the questions, explore the possible reasons why and ask yourself how you could improve.

Answer the following questions:

● What impression did I create?
● Which questions did I find it difficult to answer?
● Did I say all I wanted to say?
● What will I do differently next time?

The more you know about yourself through this form of review and other forms of feedback, the better equipped you are to present yourself to others.

Interviews are so complex and artificial as a process for all parties that, no matter how thoroughly you prepare, some may not turn out as you hope or expect. Don't dwell on the interviews that don't go well; understand why and learn from them.

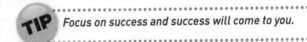

TIP *Focus on success and success will come to you.*

Feedback

Don't be afraid to ask for comments from the interviewer. If they are not offered, make a point of asking for them. If there are areas that you suspect, or are told, consistently let you down, seek help or a second opinion. Investigate local sources of help, such as:

- colleges
- business schools/universities
- guidance organizations

- professional institutes, e.g. The Chartered Management Institute in the UK
- DVDs, books and e-books
- careers counsellors
- e-learning programmes.

Don't be afraid to ask! Educational establishments are responsive to their customers and, if you have a need, approach them with it. If nothing currently exists, then why not set something up; organize an event through your local professional institute or with a group of colleagues? Practice is never wasted. Feedback and development are essential to your future success.

Above all, enjoy the experience. The most valuable interviews are frank, open discussions involving facts, ideas and opinions. By following a simple pattern, you can achieve the success you want at interviews.

Summary

You have reached the end of the week and learned what you can do to help yourself shine in interviews.

There are some simple steps to succeeding at interviews:

- Understand the interview process.
- Do your research on the interview, the role and the organization.
- Discover what differentiates you.
- Prepare yourself for success.
- Respond skilfully and be prepared for the questions and exercises.
- Decide what questions you want to ask.
- Put it all together and know that you have done all you can towards your success.

As you are very well prepared, all you need now are our best wishes and a quick reminder: the more you practise, the luckier you get.

Good luck!

Fact-check (answers at the back)

There is more than one possible answer to some of the following questions.

1. What do you need to feel confident about at interview?
   a) What you say ❏
   b) How you say it ❏
   c) That you're better dressed than the interviewer ❏
   d) You don't need to feel confident with anything about your performance at interview ❏

2. What are your objectives for the interview?
   a) To make it last as long as possible ❏
   b) To present yourself in the best possible light ❏
   c) To get through the process ❏
   d) To keep it as short as possible ❏

3. What should you concentrate on in your rehearsals?
   a) Your entrance ❏
   b) Your body language ❏
   c) What you say ❏
   d) Negative feedback. ❏

4. What should your body language be like at interview?
   a) Relaxed ❏
   b) Tense ❏
   c) Show you are paying attention ❏
   d) Giving you away ❏

5. How should your voice sound at interview?
   a) Convincing ❏
   b) Anxious to get all your information across ❏
   c) Monotonous ❏
   d) Vague ❏

6. When you receive feedback from a practice interview, what should you focus on?
   a) What you can improve ❏
   b) Where you are strong ❏
   c) The fact that they might have got it wrong ❏
   d) Things you can't change ❏

7. How do you know you are ready for the interview ?
   a) When you've rehearsed ❏
   b) When you've planned what you will wear ❏
   c) When you think you can 'wing it' ❏
   d) When you've arrived. ❏

8. When is the best time to review your performance?
   a) Immediately after the interview ❏
   b) Never; you are just happy it's over ❏
   c) When you receive feedback ❏
   d) Once you've got the job ❏

9. What areas of your performance do you need to think about before an interview?
   a) The impression you create ❏
   b) Answering questions ❏
   c) Getting across all you want to say ❏
   d) All of the above ❏

10. When is it acceptable to ask for feedback from interviews?
    a) Always ❏
    b) Sometimes ❏
    c) Never ❏
    d) If you feel it went well ❏

7 × 7

1 Seven key ideas

● **Know what to expect.** You may have to go through different stages before you come face to face with an interviewer. At each stage of the process, some candidates are sifted and do not proceed to the next stage – make sure this is not you!

● **Do your research.** The old saying 'Fail to prepare, prepare to fail' comes to mind. Your success at interviews depends on how well you understand the role, the organization and the sector.

● **Prepare yourself.** You know you will be facing tough competition, so how you look and feel are important. When you look in the mirror, what is the image you portray? You should look like a person who can perform in the role.

● **Feel confident.** Everyone has different ways of building their confidence. You may feel sure of your skills and what you've achieved to date, but you can enhance your confidence by acknowledging these and remembering the times when you've felt supremely confident.

● **Differentiate yourself.** If you are one of 20 candidates, what will make you stand out? You should understand the challenges of the role and the organization sufficiently to be the ideal candidate.

● **Respond skilfully**. How you respond to questions will distinguish you from the competition. This could include making your responses just the right length and with the right content and creatively highlighting how you will contribute to the organization.

Review your performance. Reflect on how you feel you have performed. If you have the opportunity to get feedback on your performance, take the opportunity and learn from it.

2 Seven great quotes

- 'You never get a second chance to make a first impression.' Oscar Wilde
- 'Nothing can stop the man with the right mental attitude from achieving his goal; nothing on earth can help the man with the wrong mental attitude.' Thomas Jefferson
- 'I've learned that people will forget what you said, people will forget what you did, but people will never forget how you made them feel.' Maya Angelou
- 'Your attitude, not your aptitude, will determine your altitude.' Zig Ziglar
- 'Life isn't about finding yourself. Life's about creating yourself.' George Bernard Shaw
- 'Meditate. Live purely. Be quiet. Do your work with mastery. Like the moon, come out from behind the clouds! Shine.' Buddha
- 'Life shrinks or expands in proportion to one's courage.' Anais Nin

3 Seven influential people

- **Max Eggert** is a psychologist, several of whose books are on the recommended reading lists of international universities. His work has stood the test of time.
- **Professor Steve Peters** is a consultant psychiatrist working in business, education, health, elite and Olympic sport. His specialist interest is in the working of the human mind and how it can reach optimum performance, in all walks of life.

- **Anthony Robbins** is one of the foremost authorities on the psychology of peak performance. He is the guru of personal, professional and organizational turnaround and he has been called one of the greatest influencers of his generation.
- **Dale Carnegie**, known as 'the arch-priest of the art of making friends', pioneered the development of personal business skills, self-confidence and motivational techniques.
- **Martin John Yate** is a best-selling author of books on careers and being interviewed.
- Find your own inspiration – who, in your network, has been successful at interview?
- Be your own inspiration!

4 Seven great resources

- Max Eggert, *Perfect Interview: All you Need to Get it Right First Time* (Random House, 2007) – a classic book on being interviewed
- www.interviewgold.com – a website offering fresh ideas on being interviewed
- www.myinterviewsimulator.com – a website with tough questions and answers
- www.nationalcareersservice.direct.gov.uk – a service available nationwide in the UK for jobseekers
- www.learndirect.co.uk/improve-your-job-prospects/help-getting-job/virtual-job-interview – an interactive site where you are asked questions by virtual employers and scored on your response
- www.youtube.com – many examples of being interviewed
- Richard N. Bolles, *What Color Is Your Parachute? 2015; A Practical Manual for Job-Hunters and Career-changers* (Ten Speed Press, published annually) – the world's most popular job-search book

5 Seven things to avoid

- Lack of preparation – make time to prepare thoroughly for the interview.
- Insufficient research into the organization – your research will help you understand their culture, language and the challenges for them and you in the role.
- Not understanding why you want the role – it's the simplest question but often trips people up. Make your responses authentic.
- Not answering the questions – listen to each question carefully and answer it thoroughly, addressing the question itself and not just responding with your prepared answers.
- Not selling yourself – this is your opportunity to blow your own trumpet.
- Only asking questions about salary and benefits – instead, ask questions that put you in the role, such as 'What would be your advice to me on induction?'
- Rushing – leave enough time to prepare and get there.

6 Seven key actions

- Think about yourself in the role.
- Be clear what success looks like in this role.
- Plan time to research the role and the organization further by talking to someone who knows the organization.
- Put yourself in the interviewer's shoes. What impression do you want to leave them with and how can you achieve this?
- Prepare your questions and practise your answers and say them out loud.
- Think about the impact you make at every stage of the interview process, and particularly think about your first impressions.

7 Seven trends for tomorrow

- There will be different stages to the selection process and methods of selection. More of these will be conducted virtually.
- Your interviewers will gather information on you from a variety of sources. When you put your name into a search engine, what do you find?
- Your success at interview will be as much about cultural fit as capability.
- Questions will get fewer and tougher.
- You will be more likely to have to demonstrate your achievements through examples, such as a portfolio or a presentation.
- Employers are increasing their expectations when it comes to standards of literacy.
- People who show that they can communicate and interact effectively will command an advantage.

Answers

Sunday: 1b, c; 2a; 3a; 4a, b, c; 5a, c, d; 6b; 7b; 8a, d; 9b, c; 10a, c

Monday: 1a; 2a, b, c; 3d; 4b; 5a, b; 6a, b, c; 7a, d; 8c, d; 9a, b, c; 10b, c, d

Tuesday: 1a, c, 2b, c, d; 3b, c, d; 4b, c; 5, b, d; 6a, c, d; 7a, b, c; 8a, b; 9a, d; 10a, c

Wednesday: 1a, d; 2a, b; 3a; 4b, c; 5a, b, d; 6b; 7d; 8a, b, d; 9a, b; 10a, b

Thursday: 1a, b, c; 2a, b; 3b, c; 4a, d; 5c, d; 6b; 7a, d; 8a, c; 9b; 10a, b

Friday: 1a, b; 2c; 3a, b; 4a, c, d; 5a, b, c; 6a, b, c; 7a; 8a, c; 9a, c; 10a, b

Saturday: 1a, b; 2b; 3b, c, d; 4a, c; 5a; 6a; 7a, b; 8a; 9d; 10c

ALSO AVAILABLE IN THE 'IN A WEEK' SERIES

APPRAISALS • BRAND MANAGEMENT • BUSINESS PLANS • CONTENT MARKETING • COVER LETTERS • DIGITAL MARKETING • DIRECT MARKETING • EMOTIONAL INTELLIGENCE • FINDING & HIRING TALENT • JOB HUNTING • LEADING TEAMS • MARKET RESEARCH • MARKETING • MBA • MOBILE MARKETING • NETWORKING • OUTSTANDING CONFIDENCE • PEOPLE MANAGEMENT • PLANNING YOUR CAREER • PROJECT MANAGEMENT • SMALL BUSINESS MARKETING • STARTING A NEW JOB • TACKLING TOUGH INTERVIEW QUESTIONS • TIME MANAGEMENT

For information about other titles in the 'In A Week' series, please visit
www.teachyourself.co.uk